A FIRST LOOK: COLLECTED POEMS

JIT BHATTACHARYA

Copyright © Jit Bhattacharya
All Rights Reserved.

ISBN 978-1-68563-200-7

This book has been published with all efforts taken to make the material error-free after the consent of the author. However, the author and the publisher do not assume and hereby disclaim any liability to any party for any loss, damage, or disruption caused by errors or omissions, whether such errors or omissions result from negligence, accident, or any other cause.

While every effort has been made to avoid any mistake or omission, this publication is being sold on the condition and understanding that neither the author nor the publishers or printers would be liable in any manner to any person by reason of any mistake or omission in this publication or for any action taken or omitted to be taken or advice rendered or accepted on the basis of this work. For any defect in printing or binding the publishers will be liable only to replace the defective copy by another copy of this work then available.

This collection of poems is dedicated to my maternal grandfather, the Late Shri Samar Chatterjee.

Contents

Volume 1: Home

1. Tropical Green	3
2. God(s)	5
3. To Darjeeling	8
4. Daybreak	10
5. Looking On From A Verandah	11
6. What Do You Covet?	13
7. Calcutta	14
8. Steppenwolf	17
9. Woman By A Well	18
10. A Generation	20

Volume 2: Home And Beyond

11. In The New Land	25
12. West Philly	27
13. Klaus Nomi	29
14. Steppenwolf Redux	30
15. Manhattan, 5 Months	33
16. Love And Death	35
17. Sleep	37
18. In The New Land Ii	39
19. God	43
20. Fear	44
21. Memory	45
22. What Is God	48

Contents

23. The Continuum 49

Volume 1: Home

1. Tropical Green

The green of Bengal
in the monsoon
is deep and all-pervading
It shines under a hot,
humid sun after the rains
the vivid burnished green
of paddy, sal, alstonia,
the sundari, taal, casuarina
etched with whites of
swaying Kaash flowers
It grows and nurtures
*

From the waters,
the dark loamy soil,
the rain polished leaves,
from the deep dark night
It brings out many little creatures
which crawl or buzz or flit
while some silently taste your blood
and leave their mark
You feel the twinge
*

It is ... what it is ...
Soothing pleasure sensed
with slivers of pain
mixed in

2. God(s)

If you consider God as
the sum of all things left
unexplained,
and as some of the unexplained
retracts
with new understanding and reasoning,
even as new phenomena
arise
that escape logic and expression,
*

You must have realized
the concept of God ...
Changes
and cannot be tied down to
a written Word
or a Time
or a Place
*

One could be content
with the 33 Asuras and Suras
that represent each
natural phenomena, animal
form or human emotion

*

And on the wisdom and practice
of ways to assuage
the battles raging within
the sides always changing

*

To make choices that
do good to more than oneself
and do not impose on the Kafir
with your burden

*

Question the fallout in
the 11 gods and demons
inside of you taken
to form a Godhead greater than
sum of its parts

*

Or in trying to unravel
the formlessness of
a Brahma abstract

*

You may suspect
Prajapati probably lies outside
of any human intellect

*

And the God in likeness of Man,
the crafted dogma, bias,

It's time has long passed
like a horsewhip
used to fly
an aircraft

3. To Darjeeling

Pankhabari road climbs
narrow, roughshod
winding up the hills
steep with razor turns
each side of vertical rock,
wild flowers, ferns and moss
or sheer fall to valleys
changing color, as clouds
throw moving shadows
playing with sunlight
tin-roofed huts here and there
on flat steps on the rise
man trudging up alone
in the middle of nowhere
*

The air clears, thins
forests of tall dark pines
dense, fall away down
pine cone smell in the air
takes you back many years
The mist creeps in
blurs edges and spaces
between trees,

they stand solemn sentinel
to endless mysteries

*

Sounds fall behind
it grows quiet,
so quiet....
Your muscles relax
all the postures and masks
you held up so long
fall away one by one
You wonder how
time was so wasted
chasing false prophets
how ever did it come to this...
the silence hangs immaculate
All around
Just the hum of the jeep.

4. Daybreak

I wait for...
the first moments after I awake
each and every day
before daylight strengthens
and spreads
before realization of aches and
pain, which balance
wisdom of years and intent,
is felt
*

For just those few seconds
before wind takes the flame
A slow electric ripples,
as in a child
of a sureness that
anything could be done
under a new morning sun

anything is possible....

5. Looking On From A Verandah

The white and gray cat
suddenly jerked
its head up
in a blur, bounding
up the tree trunk
leaped to lock its jaw tight
around the squirrel's neck
noiselessly climbing down
the gardener, hollering,
gave chase
the cat swiftly skirting
the edge of a water well
dropped its prey while
escaping through
the grilled iron gate
it was too late
as the man held
the scrawny, black-striped
dirt-brown squirrel
limp by its tail

And soon, the quiet of

the mid morning sun
settled back again
surely in the leafy glade
amid rustle of leaves,
cooing of pigeons
mango, magnolia
chrysanthemums in the shade

6. What Do You Covet?

I had read somewhere
Or maybe heard,
To some minor celebrity,
a final question posed,
from a rapid-fire set,
that went
"And....what do you covet? "
*

This had lingered for long,
Maybe the answer
for each of us, is...
"to take the persona of a God" ?
As we give and take hits
that diminish
us over the years
And as we came into being
as unique little gods
when we were born...
Of perfect substance and form,
We each subconsciously know
That it is, perhaps,
the only thing
We ever really lost

7. Calcutta

How..... to what pulls you, this city
through its veins, through its roots
spread, grown chaotic
its shame, its id ... obstinance
makes you feel as one, like a king
like a baby back in her womb
its passion, its senses from strong
to maudlin, the soft deceit, cowardice
veiled in cacophonic apologies
its deep rooted care surfaces languid,
lingers longer than necessary
*

This modern city born occidental
free thinkers, churned with Durga, Kali
allegorical and godless at the same instance,
halted suddenly in its tracks unbelieving
stumbling as a high bred woman raped,
sari torn hanging around her bruises
limping on high stiletto heels, eyes defiant
*

Is it the indo-gothic arcades jammed with
ramshackle colours in abstract lines
dusted vibrant... mad rush

under a hot morning sun
sweat dripping, people hanging
from door rails on dented tin buses
zig zag, here there, crowds swell
there are patterns underlying mercurial
*

Or by-lanes escaping from the noise
winding by a banyan thick trunked
ageless into the quiet of
green venetian blinds wide
facing oblong above curved terraces
half hidden by rustling leaves
wrought iron gates intricate
*

Safe haven to middle class genteel
matriarchs with translucent skin,
oiled long black hair glistening
speak in measured sweet syllables
smell of fish lightly spiced, burnt
with mango, wrapped in banana leaf
mobile hawker in the afternoon heat
hanging, gives his mournful cry
on a deserted street
*

Its anglo mixed quarters still show signs
of lounge music, pish pash
neo-classical structures lining alleys

cut up with stairs false ceilings
second hand vinyl stores tucked between
butchers, tailors, bakeries
khansamas bred in adjacent
saracen streets a little north where
live descendants of Wajid Ali

*

Or cobbled lanes snaking through
red brick warehouses by the river
hide traces of lost commerce and order
painted clay gods, hanging wires
in dark corners, where ghosts of the past
mix easily with the living, a continuum
slowly over time disappearing

*

With each passing year its stories
its secrets....its very soul
retreating into buried crevices
into a darkness invisible to many
other than a few who, like you,
know where to look
Is this how it pulls you....this city?

8. Steppenwolf

As I watch the grey skies
this balmy afternoon,
the wind nudging the trees,
drops of rain here and there,
A blood red leaf
passes me on the way
to the ground.
*

The lonely steppenwolf
prowls the earth,
and scours the grey
Deflecting another arrow
to survive
As the clouds in his eyes
sink deeper
and deeper...

to form another layer

9. Woman By A Well

She squats by the well
jet black hair knotted up tight
sari bunched around her waist
the small of her dark bare back
glistening in the hot sun
moving in fluid motion bending
forward swinging back ( ) in half circles
her shoulder blades taut ( ) against
sun-baked, dark crimson skin
undulating like black velvet sheen
oozing musky odours dense
she pounds linen on the stones wet
*

From water running, spraying jets
her conch shaped haunches full
muscles moving like pistons
in rhythm with deliberate grace
her dark angular face ( ) in half scowl
hair lip pursed in soft down
ink black eyes sharp focused
head bends down/up in short waves
the wet of armpits, spreading
under her blouse, ( ) flashes

as folds of her ample breasts shake
thud, thud, thud on the stones wet
*

Shaking off all prejudice with
each pounding she makes
She could be a housemaid,
A fruit seller, A mother,
some villager's wife dutiful & obedient
silent to most, not much education
*

But here ( ) at this time,
in this moment
she is a keeper of all that is known
and that remains unexplained
A force mighty and sensual in motion
churning a vortex all consuming
A Kali reincarnate at work
(by the stones)
in reshaping the world and its innocence

10. A Generation

We, who were born of
the dying embers of empire
with new nations clawing at
old orders on quicksand
fueled by soviet gremlins
spreading like fire to equalize
finding new meaning in
ancient texts and rituals
to stoke self-worth and pride
*

We, who were deeply ingrained with
Shakespeare, Shaw, Wordsworth
felt the beauty of traces from
a fountain pen or the tapping
of a typewriter on a new ribbon
Even as we knew of discoveries of
a new particle or a new planet
We played for a time with kaya
to turn on, tune in, and drop out
with Carroll's Caterpillar or Bankim's Cat
*

Witnessed Fabian goals come true
sprung from a faceless, a casteless

capitalism in the new land
Marked the birth of the web, the file-share
the smoke billowing from twin towers
rolling towards the Jersey shore
The rise of machines blurring focus
sedating human acts
And yet we knew deep down
a few trained elites were needed
to lead by example, to guide,
to open new doors for the rest

Volume 2: Home And Beyond

11. In The New Land

My friend Eddie from Ghana
with a state scholarship moved
to study in Moscow, Russia
he learnt the language, fell in love
with a local brunette, Yelena
she taught him ways of the land,
was devoted, protected him
from occasional taunts on his color
*

Eddie was street-smart, a hustler
he made short trips to Europe
to smuggle clothes, belts, bandanas
wearing 5-6 layers of shirts and trousers
each time he came in from the border
*

But what he really wanted was
to make a life in America
so, rather than go home after college
he promised he would bring her
to him in a few years
and bought a ticket to Philadelphia
*

Eddie and I worked parking lots downtown
ten to twelve of us valets toiled
running cars up and down
Younus, the manager, was an Afghan
who had fled with coming of the Taliban
Saye, from the Ivory Coast, worked nights
as a security guard in the suburbs
*

Mathew from Ethiopia had been
a guerrilla for Eritrean freedom
Yakov was quiet, kept to himself
he was a teacher from St. Petersburg
Genene drove a cab nights in New York
Joe was a school janitor in Germantown
*

Famata from Liberia, Eunice from South Africa
All nose-to-the-ground, hardworking people,
kept honest with no time to stray or idle
rebuilding their lives one day at a time
letting time bury what they had left behind
*

It took Eddie four years of saving,
paying a few bribes and some fretting,
before he could bring his girl Yelena
from half way around the world
to a new beginning.

12. West Philly

Boarded houses, peeled, dusty brown
broken sidewalks with ferns
between the cracks grown
check cashing van on Fridays
on to the liquor store
buxom cashier girl behind
bullet-proof glass eyes
sugar daddies after work
burly man cripple squats outside
beer shop/deli on his board
smiles polite as you walk out
if you could spare anything at all
*

black kid guards Korean store for
extra money after school
Chinese take-out joints all barred
no one in sight until you call
Teen mom dressed up, rides
gypsy cabs after dark
to buy milk for her son
makeshift table on the pavement
selling shades, incense and the Koran
*

salted hard pretzels with mustard
cheese steak with sweet peppers
and extra onions
Jewish meat fresh in a Reuben at
Koch's on 43rd and Locust
nearby Ethiopian restaurants serve
hot injeras, yebeg tibs with salad
*

musty, dank dark bar I play
Chi-Lites on the jukebox
man comes up to compliment
puts down coins for more
we talk about the funk, chasing
coors light with bourbon
Teddy, Roots, Gamble & Huff
Delfonics, Patti, Billy Paul
*

Chelten Ave or Walnut street
Baltimore ave or Cobbs Creek
the city sits easy,
unsure, a little lost
between New York and DC
but this here, brother,
is the underbelly,
the pulse
the very heart of soul....
West Philly

13. Klaus Nomi

I imagined Klaus Nomi applying lipstick,
eyeliner, upstrokes of blush on cheekbone
An aria playing in his head, while
putting on a new white and gold dress
in bated breath anticipation
for her lover's caress
*

And..
*

Passers-by on the street saw
a figure with one hand cut off,
blood dripping on a bloodied dress
the face daubed, a ghastly pale,
A freakshow hurriedly
hobbling away

14. Steppenwolf Redux

These are quicksilver days
with inchoate dread
throbbing the underbelly
in quiet waves
they pause.....
and then ascend
*

A surprising independence
uncalled maybe,
Pulls away lines of order,
purpose
Blurs stimuli
A silent osmosis drains
into bleak fogs of
not-day, not-night...
a perpetual twilight
*

Going from town to town
Temporary shelters
made temporary by
perplexed glances
cooled, solidified in dismissal,
on realization

of no barter possible
in the wolf's eyes.
*

The beast yearns for,
but cannot give nor receive,
a defined love
And yet the hunger grows
silent inner fires
rising and spreading wide
forlorn, blood red
against a gun metal sky
*

Thoughts of death come
in spasms, they come...
they pass ...
leave a sense more real
of turning skin
fading breath
closing eyes
A futile despair dims
towards acceptance
*

The wolf is cursed with
a conscience, it muddles
pure kinetic reflex
to chaos, a constant war
rages...flames...clouds....

The love remains
in tiny undercurrents
of hollowed out pain

*

I am the Steppenwolf
And these are
my quicksilver days

15. Manhattan, 5 Months

If I must...
I'd rather be sad
in New York
The dark, the grays
and tall shooting up...
closing the sky
in angles and lines
sides of granite glass
climb to spires, gargoyles
shadows in dark suits
and dresses glide
behind yellow cabs
crowds against me
at the subway turnstile
Dominican girls
dressed fine in furs
on broadway looking up
laughing under neon lights

The homeless man nods
as he bums a cigarette and
concedes with his eyes
sour smells waft by

a delivery van parked
beside an Italian restaurant
A sea of faces emerge
from the lexington subway
early morning cold bites
in seconds you stand alone
the falun gong man
protests in silence
on the sidewalk

I am looking at the woman
in the apartment across
pacing in some thought
alone
Yes I can feel snug lonely,
feel sad with many
in this crowded town
of islands lost...
Of crowded ghosts reaching out.

16. Love And Death

At what point in time
did you realize,
Accept
You...
won't live forever
let go of the sense
that death
happens to others
*

A truth you had kept on pause
while you did other things
Your ego
now released
you look around you with
new eyes , new meaning
*

The brightness of white flowers
on a frangipani tree
After the rains, the cool
earthy fragrance of a breeze
*

The antics of a lizard in the corner
stalking its prey

The beauty in motion of
a dark-skinned woman
washing clothes by the well
*

The sadness from children,
now all grown up,
living their lives far away
Loneliness at nightfall
can be harsh sometimes
but this weakness too passes
*

Time relaxed, time contracted
in the same moment
The love, selfless,
for all,
for everything around
is infinite

17. Sleep

I was thinking of Huffington's
guttural sweet voice
explaining deprivation of sleep
many years ago
and how for many, many years now,
I haven't had sleep...
that deep deep,
eight-hour straight,
uninterrupted
state of temporary death
and back to sense

*

Nowadays, it creeps in,
powders in my forehead and eyelids,
but then disappears
in a few hours I am clear-eyed
It flummoxes, oscillates,
like Heisenberg's principle
it teases,
comes and goes in waves
it leaves my head heavy in half light,
a weight I carry like a curse
through day and night

*

Do you remember the sleep
you had as a boy
no REM, no dreams to cloud,
just an instant, drop dead
passage... natural in its rebound
and when you awoke
lifted yourself up sprightly with
arms stretched back and grounded in support,
muscles bunched around shoulders, looking out
you felt the light through you
so fresh, so pure
crystal clear and strong,
so that you could move mountains
or easily take a leap to the sun?

18. In The New Land II

The first time I stepped onto the New Land,
the first time I crossed the oceans
to land in any western nation,
I was made of anglo colonial prose,
bits of sanskrit shlokas my father recited
when explaining something verbose
the burning tropical heat sweating
thousands on the streets, shoving, pulling,
without rancour, with a wink
inessant rain falling hard for 3 days straight
breaking asphalt, flooding drains
dark patches on buildings water-lime stained
flesh of ripe mango, sapodilla soft succulent
fish market cobblestones wet with scales, skins,
bones among cacophonic bargains
*

I was walking along the Skukyll expressway
people craning from car windows curious
i did not know nor understand
no one walks on a highway, my friend...
of this beautiful fall morning
leaves turning brown and yellow and red
the cold clean air heavy in apprehension

home always at the back of my head
like an earthing numbing the now to surreal
The first night I buy a packet of burgers
and on biting into a patty taste its rawness
Did I really expect a ready-to-go burger , like
those Archie comics, to pop out of this carton?
You see, I came from housemaids who
cooked and cleaned and cleared tables
who were like family, surrogate mothers
except they could not sit on the furniture;
unwriiten laws of social encryption
*

Women here jerk their arms in taut angles
stiffen their fingers into claws when talking
their eyes frank, open, non-judgemental
The Nigerian woman I used to dread
standing on the way on School House lane
explaining Jehovah's Witness; She was earnest
wearing the same soiled cream coat
with her knotted dusty hair, her dark eyes
insistent; standing there alone waiting
Did I say the first time in any western nation?
That was a lie, when I was five
we lived in England for a time
In school some called me "Blackie"
and laughed in almost a good natured way
made me feel uneasy, not yet upset

some days I didn't want to meet those boys again
*

I was from where a name marked a person,
his place, the measure of his respect
Now the name was a puzzle, sometimes a test
as a map without markings, meaningless
By Children's Hospital at the parking place
I ran up and down from street to basement
driving cars getting tips, steerings glazed
with hair oil, floor strewn with paper cups,
crumpled wrappers, hair pins
Valets from 7 countries, 4 continents drop
all their baggage behind for to run and hustle
here; second job waiting once this shift is clocked
"when you getting a real job, JB?" asks one
I learnt quickly you need to have wheels
to land a real job or earn a woman's attention
*

A Yehudi, lettered in Scriptures, revered
turned into someone to be circumspected
A Zulu warrior standing tall, majestic in pictures
turned into one wearing a baseball cap reversed
Bougainvilla, Kadamba, Frangipani gave way
to Wintergreen, Coneflower, Coral Bells, Sage
From days filled with siblings, aunts, cousins
to a loneliness like a silent volcano imploding
from the navel, pushing up softly... softly

to a freedom pushed open to a wide-screen
no questions asked, do you have the money?
And so we learned to live with each other
home loans, PTAs, landscaping lawns
Italian wedding soup, golubtsi so soft,
melting reuben at Jewish Deli on Locust
hot injera soaking up last of kitfo juices
Brooklyn Gurdwara houses 30 families
with all their belongings bundled in
blankets and bags sleeping on the floor
shuttling between two worlds lost
like a meteor hurtling in space searching

19. God

Don't talk to me of your god
unless you can show him to me
since you say we are in his form
give me proof, evidence in reality
and don't sidestep into homilies,
parables, indirect reasoning
I am as aware as you, of
ethical values and philosophy
those are man-made postulates
evolving, some tested, theories
*

I can understand god as nature,
or love... or self ... or in beauty
your elaborate codes of conduct
around your god, mean nothing to me
what does your literal god look like?
If you need to convince me
bring him or something of him here now
else, don't waste my time....please

20. Fear

Do not be afraid,
I say to myself,
as the darkness draws near
spreading like a funnel of locusts
heavy in animus
as the stomach hollows
comes a lightness in the head
a cold finger to the chest
pushing up for release
Breathe Prepare
Breathe again
Regulate your breath
There is a door that
gets around it
Not a door to escape
But a door that opens sudden
to suck it all in
and which closes shut
behind it
Forever

21. Memory

Ten or eleven years old,
lying on my bed
in the dark dorm hall
grown quiet now
after the call for 'lights out',
listening to the high-pitched
tat-a-tat-tat of rain
drumming incessant
on the metal roof above
with the cool coming in
from a jalapahar night
through turret windows
lulling me, clouding me
I sink into the drone
and trance of rainfall
*

Or even further back,
crouching low,
I am peering at
the line of ants crawling
through the grass, maneuvering
cracks and uneven soil
on the lawn, it thrills me

to imagine deep dark forests
with undulating, disappearing trails,
with swaying shadows,
half-light...hidden shapes
the revelation flowing electric,
heightened naturally for seconds

*

Or fast forward twenty years,
in a foreign land where
she was strong,
without judgment
was ready to give her all
I broke her heart
with ignorant cultural baggage
stupid, misguided fear...bias
ran away like a coward
the shame, buried fathomless,
on hearing the pain
in her voice... the surprise

*

Now, decades later
I feel the need to balance
this pull of memory flashes
with the diving forward
to something new to discover
which give child-like thrills,
far removed from

mind games or rumor
keep away those memories
from turning sour,
ferment for long
into maudlin nostalgia
the soul clock broken
directionless zombie stupor

22. What Is God

If you postulate God as
all that remains unexplained,
and as some of the unexplained retracts
with new understanding and reasoning,
even as new phenomena arise
which baffle and defy explanation,
you must have realized
the concept of God ... changes
and cannot be tied down to
a written word
or a time
or a place.

23. The Continuum

Now that you're older
moving past the faith
of god(s) and godmen
voodoo dolls, star signs
the bad loves mask
a broken science
seeds planted long
turn sins hung heavy
against your breath
*

Now you suspect
this, a continuum of
birth change decay
of the many to one
to its passing away,
and you and your mind
looking for reasons
searching for ways
*

A mind play?
yet, inside you know
to flow in rhythm
in heat and burn

a dance brings back a smile
as a child's laugh
The wonders remain
clear in soundless chants

***

Jit Bhattacharya's poetry has been published in journals such as Muse India, Bombay Review, and, Indian Ruminations. He graduated with a Master's degree in Decision Science from Drexel University, Philadelphia. Jit lives and works in Kolkata, India.

www.ingramcontent.com/pod-product-compliance
Lightning Source LLC
LaVergne TN
LVHW041544060526
838200LV00037B/1138